DREAM BIG

But

BEWARE of DREAM KILLERS

TODD WILSON

ISBN-13: 978-0-9821941-5-7
ISBN-10: 0-9821941-5-3

Printed in the United States of America

This book is for you.
Do it.

This is the third time I've started this book. The previous drafts began with flowery stories of historical, Biblical, and modern-day dreamers. It's not that they weren't brilliantly written, but to be honest, they seemed a little sappy and lacked...punch. Then I got an email from Mark which cleared my head and clarified my vision.

Here's what he wrote:

> *Hey Todd,*
> *Getting a little vulnerable here, but I need some encouragement.*
> *About 3am this morning my son (9) comes downstairs and crawls into bed with us. There was probably no reason other than a full bladder that woke him, but he would rather be with us than alone. He decides to share my pillow this time rather than my wife's. I looked at his face and my first thought is...He needs me. I need to be at home.*

Fast forward 2 hours to my quiet time, and I can't focus on my bible study because this drive to be home haunts me. It takes so much effort to be faithful at work when the desire is to be somewhere else—home. But what does this look like? What do I need to make the change?

I cry (real tears) to the Lord:

Jesus, fulfill this desire or take it away. It is difficult to carry.

I don't want to be a fool but how do I step out in faith?

Lord, you know what my mind and personality needs, give me more clarity. Time moves. I am losing time. Please do something, Jesus, please.

The emotional release helped and I pulled myself back together and press on. The problem is press on in what? Doing something part time while holding a full time job defeats what I want to accomplish. I don't have enough direction to quit the day job. In the same way I think welfare has blinded and trapped the poor of our country, so too I think the traditional workplace had blinded and trapped me. I'm getting dramatic, I know...

I'm sorry to dump on you. I welcome any thoughts or help.

~Mark

Suddenly I feel invigorated and flush with passion. Mark's right. Time is against him, consuming decades in the blink of an eye. It's obvious to me that God has indeed placed a dream in his heart, but if he fails to act on it, time will consume him and then spit out his bones as a trophy and reminder of its power.

And believe me, time has plenty of trophies on its shelf in the form of millions of men and women in whom God placed a dream deep in their hearts but for one reason or another failed to step out in faith and achieve those dreams. History fails to record their stories because they chose to live safe, ordinary lives, spending their remaining days killing the dreams of others.

Put simply, there are just two kinds of people: dreamers and used-to-be-dreamers. To me, there is no sadder statement. That's why I'm starting this book again...because it needs to be written and you need to read it and then step out in faith and DREAM BIG!!!!

The 'safe' people around you will shake their heads in disbelief. Well-meaning, 'safe' Christians will quote 'safe' verses and encourage you to stay in the 'safe' shallows, not realizing that God wants you in deep water. He wants you to trust Him and fear nothing. He has placed a dream in your heart because he wants you to go for it, set your jaw in determination, throw caution to the wind, and do it.

The Bible is filled with dreamers who, against all odds and common sense, believed God and did something worth recording. In fact, their stories were recorded for us and serve as a reminder, not of great men, but of normal men and women who were used by a great God to do great things.

We read their familiar stories often, but somehow I think we've forgotten them. Do you remember the two dreamers, Joshua and Caleb, who believed God could conquer the land filled with giants even when the odds were against them?

How about Daniel who dared to pray to God when everyone else played it safe?

Then there are those 12 guys who left everything behind to follow a man they believed was the Messiah and even God. Their life was hard, their ending painful....but they were dreamers.

A SHIP IN HARBOR IS SAFE
- BUT THAT IS NOT WHAT
SHIPS ARE FOR.

~JOHN A. SHEDD

I've read of others, like Gladys Aylward and Bruce Olsen, who went to terrible places just to tell others about Jesus. Instead of cheers of praise, they were told that they weren't qualified or lacked what was needed. Did that stop them? No way. They were dreamers and God-inspired dreamers can't be easily stopped.

Every story worth telling had a man or woman behind it who dreamed big. Their names have become part of our vocabulary... names like Bell, Ford, Edison, Lincoln, Disney, and hundreds more.

I even heard ape-lady Jane Goodall on the radio the other day talking about when she first wanted to live among the apes. As a child she read the book Tarzan and afterwards told people that she wanted to live in Africa among the animals and write about them. Everyone laughed at her silly idea...except her mother.

But don't think for one minute that I'm only talking about famous people or people who did great things for society. I'm talking about DREAMERS. Some of the greatest dreamers were not inventors or movers and shakers but homemakers, fathers, mothers, men, and women who dared to be fools in the eyes of the world.

I meet modern-day dreamers on the road from time to time. I talk to men who have quit high-paying jobs to spend more time with their families, couples who believe all children are a blessing from God and are letting Him determine how many they have, and women who believe they can teach their children at home.

My own father is a dreamer, although he would never use that word to describe himself. He left a respectable teaching position to start a little print shop, in our little town, in our little garage, to better meet the needs of his growing family. As a kid I didn't realize how scary that was, but I remember my grandfather, who was also a teacher, telling him he thought it was a big mistake.

I'm sure others told him that as well. But you know what? He didn't listen to them. He stepped out into the deep waters and God took care of him. Oh, his business never grew into a huge mega print shop, but the shop provided for our family, gave him time to be part of our lives, and allowed him to impact many lives in the town where I grew up.

There are many other dreamers as well. In fact, your home is filled with dreamers. Your children came into the world dreaming big. All children do. They want to be ballerinas, cowboys, astronauts, and basketball players. They don't know it yet, but their dreams will soon be replaced with more realistic thinking. They will be told, "You're not tall enough, good enough, rich enough, smart enough." They won't believe it at first...but after years of being bombarded by 'common sense' they will cave in and assume their place among the used-to-be dreamers.

If a child happens to grow up in a Christian home, his odds of becoming a full-fledged dreamer are even less. Christians, who should be the biggest dreamers of all, are usually the safest people. They sit in their safe churches, listen to safe sermons, and live safe, comfortable lives.

They've become dream killers, taking it upon themselves to be the voice of reason that tells others why their dreams won't work.

Let me tell you a story of a dreamer and a dream killer... dressed only in a towel and a smile.

Shoot Out in the...Shower Room

I was getting ready one morning, minding my own business when I witnessed a murder...the murder of a dream.

To back up just a bit, let me set the scene. I was attending a writer's conference at Wheaton College with a couple hundred wanna-be-writers who had gathered to get pumped up and to schmooze with big whigs in the publishing industry. Each day was packed with workshops, special speakers, and appointments with the "publishing gate-keepers."

Trying to keep costs down, most of the attendees stayed in the host college dorm, just a few blocks away from the meeting hall. It felt like a blast from the past because it had been a long time since I had showered with a bunch of guys. In fact, it was a little unnerving, but it did change my perspective on big-whig publishers. Once you've seen the head of a big publishing house dressed only in...nothing, you never think of them the same.

With that background, I'm ready to tell you the rest of the murder story. The morning was clear and the sun bright. It had the makings of a perfect day. I was up early trying to get a jump on the rest of the shower takers and stumbled down to the dorm bathroom.

I wasn't the only one who was trying to get a jump on the day. There were several others, but I found an empty shower stall and the water was still hot. Afterwards, I stepped up to a long row of sinks and proceeded to shave.

Enter the unsuspecting victim.

He was a young guy, probably in his early twenties. I caught

OF ALL THE PEOPLE I
HAVE EVER KNOWN, THOSE
WHO HAVE PURSUED THEIR
DREAMS AND FAILED HAVE
LIVED A MUCH MORE
FULFILLING LIFE THAN
THOSE WHO HAVE PUT
THEIR DREAMS ON A SHELF
FOR FEAR OF FAILURE.

~AUTHOR UNKNOWN

his eye and smiled an "I'm shaving and don't really want to talk" kind of smile. Apparently he didn't understand 'smile-ese' because he took it as an invitation to strike up a conversation.

"How old are you?" he squeaked.

"38," I answered.

"Wow, I thought you were my age." He responded, hoping he wasn't the only 'kid' at the conference.

"*I like the way this kid thinks,*" I thought. "*Obviously he's a lot better judge of youthfulness than say...my wife and kids.* "So what kind of stuff do you like to write?" I asked.

His eyes sparkled as he launched into his dream. As he was talking, a guy dressed only in a towel, fogged up glasses, and a big smile stepped around the corner. His slick, brill-creamed hair was parted to one side and he had obviously been listening to our conversation.

Without being invited to join, he piped in, "That's fine that you want to be a writer, but you need to get a real job as well."

The young kid was stunned but smiled faintly to acknowledge that he had listened. This guy wasn't finished. He hadn't imparted all he knew about writing yet.

"Yeah, did you hear Bob Miller talk yesterday about how he still has to have a 'real' job? And he's published several books." The guy smiled a big, toothy smile, and I would have bet the farm that he was a deacon on some church board.

The young guy was against the ropes.

"Yeah, that's what you need to do first. Get a job," the smiling deacon said as his 1970's, fogged-up glasses slid down his nose.

The young man smiled and thanked the man for the advice,

and we walked out of the bathroom. So did Deacon Jones. He wouldn't back down and followed the bleeding young writer into the hallway.

"You might even think about going to work for a local news-paper or writing for your church's newsletter..."

We parted and I stepped into my room to get dressed, but my blood was starting to boil, and I had half a mind to go out and pop the good deacon in his gleaming chops.

"The guy's a dream killer," I said rather loudly to no one. "A big smiling, good motives, godly dream killer, and he just killed another dream...a young, bright, full of hope dream."

Later that day I was sitting in the front of the big auditorium when I looked towards the back and saw the 'kid' standing in the doorway.

I got up, made my way to where he stood, and asked, "So you want to be a writer, huh? What would you like to write?"

Reluctantly, he shared that he wanted to write for people in jail and then began to sob deeply. Between sniffs he told me that he had spent some time behind bars and wanted to write to those who are in similar predicaments.

I listened and that same rage that I felt early that morning toward the deacon in the towel filled my heart. When the kid was finished, I said boldly, "If you want to be a full-time writer, then you should do it. Don't listen to that guy back in the shower. He doesn't know what he's talking about."

The kid sniffed away his tears, but I was already on a roll. "I'm a full time writer," I told him (now I didn't have the heart to tell him I could have made more money picking up aluminum cans by the side of the road), and you can do it too!"

A smile replaced the tears, and I thought, "Wow, words are powerful things. They have the power to kill dreams or to fan them.

As I made my way to my seat, I wondered how many other dreams had been killed that weekend by well-meaning people? I realized then that it was my job to sound the alarm and to equip people to do battle with dream killers, because we all face them.

They look you in the eye and offer a dozen reasons why your dreams won't work. In fact, the more they talk, the more you begin to hear your own voice echo their thoughts.

Truth is, wherever you find dreamers, you find dream killers. The church is filled with them. They grew up with you, live in your house, and sometimes they...are you. Maybe you're a victim of a dream killer and regret having listened to them.

At the same time, I realize the life-giving power of dream fanners. They refresh you, and you feel drawn to them like moths to a flame.

It is my desire through this book to revive old dreams, give you the tools to counter dream killers, show you how to fan the dreams in others' lives, and see you step out in faith to achieve the dreams that God has placed in your heart.

So, take courage, brace yourself, and let's look at a well-known story about a dreamer, a dream, and some mighty frightening dream killers.

MOST PEOPLE LIVE AND
DIE WITH THEIR MUSIC
STILL UNPLAYED. THEY
NEVER DARE TO TRY.

~MARY KAY ASH

David and the Dream Killers

If you were to take a quick poll among Christians and ask them what the most famous account in the Bible is, I'm just about sure they would name the story of David and Goliath.

It's got all the makings of a great movie...a big, bad guy, insurmountable odds, and a triumphant, Rocky-type ending. You know it as the story of David and Goliath. I call it the account of David and the Dream Killers.

That's what it's really about—a guy with a big dream who encounters a pack of dream killers.

First Samuel 17 tells the account. Instead of reading the passage directly from the Bible, let me just tell you the story in my words.

Put your imagination cap on and picture a wide valley with two large armies gathered on opposite hillsides. For forty days the Israelites and Philistines gathered to do battle. They donned their armor, flashed their spears, pounded their drums, hollered threats, and called on their gods. King Saul watched from a safe distance in all his glory, ready to lead the charge...from the rear.

As though instructed to do so, the armies hushed, and from the ranks of the Philistines out stepped the Champion, Goliath of Gath. At a time when most men stood five and a half feet tall this monster stood almost ten feet tall. A javelin was slung across his back, and in his hand he carried a spear with a large, jagged point that could be seen clear across the valley.

Knowing that all eyes were upon him, Goliath arrogantly crossed the valley and came to a stop within earshot of the Israelite army. The giant inhaled deeply and roared, "Who will come and fight me?!!!"

Now at this point most of you with young children are picturing a large pickle wearing red boxing gloves as portrayed on Veggie Tales. Get that image out of your head. This was definitely NOT a Larry and Bob moment.

In my words...

"Choose a man from your side," Goliath shouted, "to come and fight me on the battlefield. If I kill him (which I plan to do) you will serve us, but if he kills me (and there's not a snowball's chance in Hell that will ever happen), then we will serve you."

Seeing that no one answered his challenge, the giant spit venom and jeered, "Come on, I defy all of you...give me a man and let us FIGHT!!!!"

In response, the Bible says that Saul and all the Israelites were dismayed and trembled. The giant returned to his army, only to repeat the whole routine all over again in the evening.

For forty days this took place. They played battle. They dressed up, sharpened their weapons, and then went to bed, only to get up and repeat it all in the morning. I guess they'd still be doing it today had it not been for...a dreamer.

Jesse's Sons

Thirty miles away from the battlefield in the small village of Bethlehem lived Jesse, an old man with eight sons. The three oldest and biggest of his boys followed Saul to war and played battle along with the rest of the Israelites.

Since these were the days before email, cell phones, and facebook, Jesse wondered how things were going for his sons and summoned his youngest son David who was out caring for their sheep to go check on the boys. "Take some food," he said to David, "and see how they are faring...and make sure you change your clothes before you go (my imagination)."

The next morning David headed out to the battlefield. After a long journey, you can imagine the excitement David must have felt as he entered the camp. Now, we don't know how long it took him to locate his brothers, but after some time David saw the boys assembled with the rest of the army and made his way to them.

I can just imagine he was about to say, "Hey guys..." when the army grew quiet and a voice boomed once again across the valley.

"Who will come and fight me?" the voice shouted. David turned to see the biggest man, if he could be called a man, that he had ever seen. The giant finished his spiel and instantly God put a dream into David's heart. "*David, I want you to kill the giant.*"

The Birth of a Dream

That's how it often is with dreams. They sneak up on you and seemingly come from nowhere at the oddest times. David didn't sit on the side of the bed that morning thinking to himself, "Man, I'd like to kill a giant today...wonder where I can find one?"

No. He was just going about his father's business when God planted the dream within him. Some of you know what that feels

I HAVE LEARNED OVER
THE YEARS THAT WHEN
ONE'S MIND IS MADE UP,
THIS DIMINISHES FEAR;
KNOWING WHAT MUST
BE DONE DOES AWAY
WITH FEAR.

~ROSA PARKS

like, don't you? Can you remember where you were when you first entertained the idea of starting a business, having another child, becoming a missionary, going back to school, adopting a child, or attempting some other cock-a-mamy idea?

For Jane Goodall, British primatologist, ethologist, and anthropologist, her dream hit her after reading Tarzan of the Apes. I've heard missionaries say that they got the dream as they listened to another missionary tell of the needs of a specific people group. I know parents to whom God whispered in their hearts as they lay in their bed staring up at the dark ceiling.

For me, it was a gentle and gradual feeling that there was something 'different' I was supposed to do. The thing about dreams is that they sound a little crazy because that's the defining factor of a God-shaped dream. It sounds about as ridiculous to the rest of the world, and oftentimes the dreamer, as a young boy fighting...a giant.

My Dream vs. God's Dream

This is the perfect time to do some dream evaluating. I hear this question often: How do I know that what I'm thinking and feeling is from God? Maybe it's just my dream and not His.

I'm afraid I can't offer you a dream-ometer that lets me punch a few buttons and say for certainty, "Yes, this dream is indeed from God." But I do know that God isn't some kind of keep-us-guessing god.

I also know it's not as difficult as some make it out to be. I believe there are a few principles that can help us determine if the "dream" you're feeling is from God or just one of your own selfish desires.

Let's look back at the account of David and the Dream killers. I think it's significant that when David got the dream he was in obedience to his father, which gives us our first principle.

1. Am I in obedience to my father? - When I talk with teenagers about their dreams for the future this is what I emphasize. Are they in obedience to not only their heavenly father but also their earthly parents?

I'm just sure David stayed behind when his brothers went to war because he was asked to stay behind. He was a fighter and loved war. It probably came as a blow when Jesse said, "Not you son. I need you to stay home and watch the sheep."

The sheep? How exciting is that? bet David would have rather worn armor than sheep poop. But David obeyed...and stayed. We don't know how long he stayed, and God didn't give away the ending on the first day by whispering in his heart, "David, don't worry. I've got big plans for you. In fact, in a while you're going to save the day by killing a giant."

Day after day, David got up, put on his poopy sheep clothes, and headed out to the field to watch sheep, all the while thinking about battle. Then one day, he got the call, not to head off to war but to take some food and bring back news of his brothers.

Still, no dream. But David obeyed, left the sheep with the head shepherd, and went to the battlefield.

For a teenager, this means that he needs to be in a right relationship with his parents. He can't be thumbing his nose at his father's warnings and mother's desires and then think that the passion he has in his heart is from God.

About a year ago, I was speaking at a conference in Michigan when a handsome young man stepped up to me and began sharing his dream of becoming a fashion designer. As he spoke, I already knew what his parents were thinking.

A fashion designer?!! Do you know what kind of men become fashion designers?!! They wear high heels and wrap pink feather boas around their necks and spend most of their days flitting around half-naked women!!!!

The young man was thoughtful and seemed to want to do the right thing, and I could tell his parents were as excited about his idea as I would have been.

"This is a tough one," I thought.

"So what do you think?" he asked.

We spent the next few minutes talking about his parent's fears and concerns. "Obey your parents," I said in desperation. "Submit to their desires and listen to their warnings. Find an avenue of fashion that pleases God and a lifestyle that does also. Do it God's way, and He will make it clear.

The truth is you can't spend your days flitting around half-naked women and living a lifestyle that flies in the face of all that is right and believe that that's what God would have you do. He does not ask us to do anything that would violate a godly principle or diminish His holiness or our purity.

"I believe God has put something about design and fashion in your heart, but you must do it his way or set the dream aside until He makes it clear how you can pull it off in a godly way."

THE BRAVE MAY NOT LIVE
FOREVER, BUT THE CAUTIOUS
DO NOT LIVE AT ALL!

Sometimes when you'd rather be fighting battles, you have to tend sheep and wait until God says, "Go."

The same principle can be applied to adults. If your dream or passion directly or indirectly violates God's principles, then your dream is not God's dream for you...right now.

I have many men tell me they have the dream of starting a new business or career, but it will mean putting in a lot of hours at first or having to work and go to school at the same time.

I know what this kind of dream will mean for these men's families. They will suffer from his absence. After all, a dad is supposed to be the head...and he can't be the head, train his children, and love his wife as Christ loves the church, if he's gone all the time.

To pursue this kind of dream, a man needs to figure out how to do it without sacrificing his family because God would not give him a dream at his family's expense.

Some argue about missionaries who sacrifice their families for the sake of their ministry, but God didn't ask them to neglect their families. He made them fathers and husbands and told them to care for the needs of their families.

God's dreams include families. If you feel like God has called you to travel for your work then you need to find a way to include your family in your travels, or tend the sheep until you can or until you don't have a family anymore.

I've had women tell me, "I have the dream of homeschooling my children...but my husband is against it."

"God wants you to love your husband," I say. "You can't do that by going against his wishes. You may have to spend some time tending the sheep until God says to homeschool."

It's really that simple...and hard.

Pull out your dream right now and take a good long look at it and answer the following:

—Am I walking in obedience to God and to others right now?

—Is my dream forbidden by Scripture?

—By doing it, will I violate a scripture mandate or principle?

—By pursuing it, will I be able to fulfill my duties to my spouse and children? Will it be good for my family, not only in the long run but in the short-run as well?

Now let's look at the second principle:

2. Is my dream crazy? - Does your dream make sense or does it look almost impossible? For Goliath, it made sense to be a warrior and challenge people in battle. He was ten feet tall for goodness sake!!! He was born for battle. David on the other hand, wasn't a weenie, but his idea of fighting a giant certainly didn't make a lot of sense to anyone but David and God.

That's the tell-tale signs of a dream from God. It sounds plain crazy when you say it out loud. And, you'll hear comments like these:

"You want to do what?"

"Do you know how many people have tried that and failed?"

"What are you, nuts?!"

"You can barely afford the kids you have now, why would you want another?

"Do you know how much it costs to adopt?"

"You want to start a home business in this economy?"

"Do you know how much college costs now-a-days?

"You're NOT going to send your kids to college?

That's the only way to succeed in life."

"You're going to take your family to the jungle to share Jesus with savages?"

"You plan to travel the country in an RV with eight children?"

Man, those all sound like responses to real, true-blue, grade A, God-sized dreams, the kind that either God will accomplish or they can't be accomplished. Those are the dreams that make people shiver when they hear them...and admire the dreamer for attempting them.

I'll never forget a man named Johnny Woods. I only met him once when he came to the small church I was pastoring in Northern Indiana. He contacted our church to see if he could present his opportunity to work on a Native American mission telling people about Jesus.

I can remember him standing up on the platform with his family. He was about as non-charismatic as a guy could be. He stumbled his way through a scripture reading and a poorly organized sermon.

His presentation had about as much pizzazz as a potato...no butter. In fact, he reminded me of a sad, old, hound dog. I'm sure there isn't a person who was there that night who even remembers him or his words, and they were probably glad when the service ended.

But I remember that night because I thought then as I do now, *if there was ever a man whom God could use and get all the glory, it would be Johnny Woods.*

A LIFE SPENT MAKING
MISTAKES IS NOT ONLY
MORE HONORABLE BUT
MORE USEFUL THAN A LIFE
SPENT IN DOING NOTHING.

~GEORGE BERNARD SHAW

You see, it's not really a dream for a tall, athletic guy to play basketball...it just makes sense. It's not uncommon for a rich guy to buy an expensive car...it just makes sense. It is not unimaginable for a godly, single, Charismatic guy to become a missionary...it just makes sense.

Now don't get me wrong, those are all fine things to do and God is still the accomplisher, but they're not necessarily God-sized dreams. And a dream doesn't even have to be a "great thing."

I know one dreamer who just wanted to have a regular 9-5 job so he could spend more time with his family. He had no big plans other than to live a peaceful life. Believe me, that's a real dream in this world that we live in because, men are supposed to want to accomplish big things, conquer countries, and climb ladders, not lead quiet lives.

So ask yourself, "Does my dream sound crazy?" If it does and you've answered all the questions above correctly, it's probably from God. But let's look at one more thing.

3. A track record - This last criterion is the least important...but it's still important. We'll talk about it a little later when we get there in the story, but at one point David finds himself standing before King Saul.

Saul is skeptical about the young guy before him and David whips off his resume. "*I know you're concerned about me killing this giant, but I do have some experience. In fact, God delivered me from the paw of the lion and the paw of the bear...and he can deliver me from the hand of this big, hairy goomer with the loud mouth.*"

I've had men and women come up to me and tell me their dreams and to be honest, I've thought, *how do you expect to do "such and such" when you've never even done it for one second.* But that's not to say that God can't accomplish what He wants to do with whom he wants to use.

I guess God *could have* taken a three-year-old little girl armed only with a jump rope and killed Goliath, but that's not usually how He works.

Here's what I'm getting at.

If your dream is starting a computer business from your home, then you ought to be able to work with computers.

If you want to be a full-time writer, then you probably ought to be writing already and had something published or gotten some positive feedback from a few people.

If you're going to have another child, you should have...a spouse.

Yes, God gives crazy dreams...but He often gives them to those who are willing and able. I hope this doesn't sound contradictory to the previous point because it isn't.

God is Bigger Than a Dumb Dream

So how does your dream stack up now? Still not sure? Be of good courage because God is the fail-safe. The last and most important thing to remember is that God kills dumb dreams.

If your dream isn't from Him, and you've asked him to stop you if it isn't, then he'll stop you. You just act in faith and pray,

"God it sure looks like this dream is from you so I'm going to assume that it is. If I'm wrong, please stop me before I hurt myself or anyone else."

Talk about taking away the pressure. Now you've got the freedom to dream, knowing that your dream is from God and that if it isn't, He's bigger than you or your dumb dreams. Unfortunately, most people never get this far. Most never act on their dreams, and their dreams are soon replaced by regrets.

But not me...not you...and not David.

David Meets a Dream Killer

"So what will be done for the guy who kills this giant?" David asked the soldiers standing near him. They informed David of all the king's perks for dispatching the giant, and Eliab, David's oldest brother, slowly became aware that the person who was talking about killing the champion was his kid brother...DAVID!

Flushed with rage, Eliab put on his dream killer hat and like the deacon in the towel, jumped on the dreamer like a buzzard on a gut-wagon.

"What...what are you doing here??!" Eliab asked. "I know you. You just came down to see the battle...you probably just walked away from your responsibilities and our sheep...you have no business talking about killing giants!!!!!!"

It's interesting to me that the first dream killer David encountered was from his own family, because that's how it often is. The people who should give us the most encouragement usually become the greatest source of discouragement.

TWENTY YEARS FROM
NOW YOU WILL BE MORE
DISAPPOINTED BY THE THINGS
YOU DIDN'T DO THAN BY THE
ONES YOU DID. SO THROW OFF
THE BOWLINES, SAIL AWAY
FROM THE SAFE HARBOR.
CATCH THE TRADE WINDS
IN YOUR SAILS. EXPLORE.
DREAM. DISCOVER.

~ MARK TWAIN

Oftentimes, when God gives you a dream, the kind and encouraging people in your family will do a quick Jekyll and Hyde transformation into dream-killing, bubble-busting, candle-snuffing wet blankets.

It might be your mother-in-law, father, husband, wife, or best friend. They will smile at you and even offer biblical wisdom...intent on killing your dream. Some do it to be mean and to keep you down; others really think they are helping you. There are reasons people act the way they do, let's look at some of them now.

Dream Killers Mean Well

Let's not be too hard on Eliab, David's older brother, or the dream killers in your life. They are, after all, just doing what they've learned over the years. They were dreamers once too but fell victim to the dream killers in their lives.

In this age of labeling...they're victims...victims of dream-murder. In fact, you ought to feel sorry for Eliab and the dream killers in your life because they usually have your best interest in mind. Like timid mice, they don't want to see you killed on the battlefield or go through a difficult time.

They don't see themselves as dream killers at all but view themselves as the voice of reason. They pride themselves on being wise and safe—saving for a rainy day, counting the cost, being prepared, or expecting the worst. They quote scripture and pray for your wisdom...but if you listen to them, they will kill the dream God has given you.

Even Jesus, as he was about to fulfill the greatest dream of all, was surrounded by well-meaning dream killers (Matthew 16:21-23). As the day drew near to the cross, Peter, one of his closest friends, pulled Him aside and 'rebuked' him for saying such things about being rejected, suffering, and dying. "God forbid it, Lord!" Peter cried. "This will never happen to you...come on, think positive."

Jesus, seeing who was behind Peter, said to him, "Get behind me Satan! You're a dream killer; for you are not setting your mind on God's dream...but man's fear." (My version).

Now Peter meant well. He didn't want Jesus to suffer and die. He wanted Jesus safe, but the truth is dreamers and dreams are never safe.

Dream Killers Admire Dreamers

I'd go as far as to say that at the same time a dream killer is trying to kill your dream, they also admire you deeply for daring to dream. In fact, I think they feel guilty for not having the gumption and bravery that you do.

I'm sure it was that way for David's brother Eliab. If you know your Bible well, you'll remember that Eliab was the biggest and best of all Jesse's boys. When Samuel was out looking for the new king to take the place of Saul he was awestruck by Eliab's appearance and thought to himself, "If ever there was a guy meant to be a king, it is Eliab!" (1 Samuel 16:6).

So just try to imagine how Eliab felt when David was talking about killing the giant while he had acted like a sniveling coward for the last forty days.

I'm sure he thought, *David's just a kid. I'm the one who should be out there battling giants. I'm the biggest, strongest, and oldest, and yet here I am hiding with the rest of these bozos while David, the youngest of Jesse's sons, wants to fight him.*

I've felt that way before. A few years ago we drove the Familyman Mobile out to Colorado Springs, CO. A highlight for us flatlanders was the Royal Gorge. It was breathtaking as we walked across a swaying suspension bridge a thousand feet above the canyon floor.

The kids didn't mind at all. They climbed the flimsy rail and peered down. I stayed pretty much in the center of the bridge and hoped it wouldn't collapse. I'm guessing that wasn't scary enough for the average tourist so the management at the Royal George decided to place a giant swing on the edge of the gorge.

It was one of those swings where the rider lays down in a sling-like contraption and is pulled backwards to the top and then...zip. The swinger free falls in a large arc out over the face of the gorge, screaming his/her lungs out. I get chills just thinking about it.

As we watched some crazy people do the swing, one of my younger sons, Ike (who was seven at the time) said, "Can I do that, Dad?"

"No, you can't do that!" I shot back. "Do you know how scary that would be?"

He obviously didn't and looked about as nervous as if he was asking to eat toast.

"I'll go with you, Ike," his brave mother piped in.

This was too much, and I forbade them for a variety of reasons like cost...cost...and cost. Truthfully, I forbade them because I felt

DREAMS AND DREAMERS
ARE NEVER SAFE!

~TODD WILSON
(A.K.A. *THE FAMILYMAN*)

ashamed that they were braver than I. Instead of just saying, "It scares me...but go for it," I acted mean and irrational giving flimsy answers to their requests. I even tried to put fear (unsuccessfully) into their hearts.

I think that is one of the main reasons why dream killers do what they do. They hate that they're scared to dream but too ashamed to admit it, and they hope that by keeping you from doing your dream it will de-emphasize their fears.

And like me, they hate themelves for doing it. I still feel ashamed that I robbed my son of a thrill of a lifetime. More importantly, maybe I even diminished his ability to dream in the future.

Nobody Likes a Dream Killer

Let me ask you a question: How do you feel towards dream killers? You don't feel very warm and fuzzy, right? In fact, you probably do all you can to avoid them.

My wife and I have experienced dream killers firsthand. I think we've spent most of our married life dreaming bold, crazy dreams. Some folks just don't understand. They warn us, tell us horror stories, shake their heads in dismay, and show obvious displeasure in their faces.

The temptation is to keep all our dreams to ourselves, holding the people we love so much at arm's distance. We've determined not to do so...but I'm pretty sure there is some residual effect and that we don't share our hearts like we should and desire to...or like they would desire us to.

But that's what happens between dreamers and dream killers. Walls are built, complete with moats and alligators. Relationships are hindered and communication breaks down.

Want to hear something really scary? Sometime *we are* the dream killers in our spouse's and children's lives...and guess how they feel towards us?

I've Seen the Dream Killer and it's Me

Back in the old days before the invention of the VCR (which is like a pre-DVD player), people went to the movies. I remember the excitement of standing in line to see the sequel to the epic movie Star Wars.

The movie was everything we had anticipated, and for a few hours we were whisked far, far away to a jungle planet where we met the ancient, puppet-like, Jedi Master, Yoda. His job was to take the young Luke Skywalker to the next Jedi level. About halfway through the movie, Luke had his first 'test.'

Drawn into a murky, dream-like place, he found himself face to face with the big bad guy of the galaxy, Darth Vader. Shocked to find Vader in this desolate place, he drew his light saber, and for a few seconds the two slashed at each other with beams of light and that familiar deep, throbbing sound that light sabers make.

Then, with one fell slash, Luke lopped off Darth Vader's head and the entire movie crowd gasped as the black helmeted head bounced and rolled right into our viewing laps. With a shower of sparks, the helmet cracked and exposed the face behind the mask.

To Luke's horror (as well as ours), he saw his own pale face with unblinking eyes.

I'm not sure about all the symbolism, but in the words of some old comic strip character named Pogo, "We've seen the enemy and it is me." In other words, we unwittingly and sometimes unknowingly become...the dream killers.

Married to a Dream Killer

I know this can be especially true for wives. In fact, I'd go as far as to say that wives can often be stereotyped as dream killers. That doesn't mean every wife kills the dreams of her husband, but a whole lot of them do.

To compound the problem, many women are married to dreamers of the worst sort. They have a dream a day...and they're all far-fetched.

Here's an example:

"Hey, Honey," the husband says with a sparkle in his eye, "I've got a great idea."

One look at the sparkle and the wife already knows she's not going to like it.

"What?" she says trying to sound somewhat interested.

Like a light saber, the husband draws out his great idea and throws it out to his wife. "So what do you think?" He asks breathless with excitement.

Long pause.

"You're kidding, right?" she says like he just suggested they

PROGRESS ALWAYS
INVOLVES RISKS. YOU
CAN'T STEAL SECOND BASE
AND KEEP YOUR FOOT ON
FIRST.

~FREDERICK B. WILCOX

fly to the moon. "There is no way we can do that...do you know how much that would cost? I'm not doing that. No way!"

The husband blows it off and agrees, but inside he feels like he just got whacked in the face by a dream killer and deep inside he resents her.

I see this happen all the time. I talk about this all over the country, and I see husbands nod their heads in agreement. My buddy, Steve and I were talking one time when he said, "My wife said she can never encourage me."

"Really? Why not?" I asked. "Because she said that if she encourages me one time...she's afraid that I'll just RUN WITH IT," he answered.

We both laughed at the thought, knowing that ALL his dreams are big and scary.

But as we laughed, I also thought, how sad. All Steve wanted to hear from his wife was, "Go for it...if anyone can do it, I know you can." That's what all husbands want to hear from their wives

I love those words. They taste good and I savor them, replaying them over in my mind. Those words from my lovely dream fanner empower, invigorate and draw me towards her. But when we husbands hear dream killing words, it does just the opposite. It pushes us away and breeds resentment and withholding. After all, how much is shared with a dream killer?

You want to know a secret to a happy marriage? Be a dream fanner. When your spouse shares those crazy dreams say, "Go for it, Babe!!! You can do it. I'm with you." There isn't a man or woman alive who wouldn't kill for a spouse like that.

Now I know what you're thinking ladies, "Yeah, but what if my husband wants to sell the house and move to Iceland to sell swimming pools? Am I supposed to fan those ridiculous dreams?"

The answer is YES!!! But remember that God kills dumb dreams. Oftentimes a guy gets a big dream, talks about how he's going to do it, and then after a couple of weeks never mentions it again. But if you fan your dreaming husband, he will love you, share more dumb dreams with you, and draw close to you. That is the power of a dream fanner.

I know this power because my dad is a dream fanner. He always has been, but at a time when I needed him most, he pulled through with flying colors.

Eight years ago, I was pastoring a small church in northern Indiana but both my wife and I felt like God was moving us into something else. We weren't exactly sure what that was, but it had something to do with writing. We had a vague plan of how we would proceed and had a small track record with some "experts" telling us we had what it took.

It was a scary time for us, and I wanted my dad's advice. So I called him and asked him to meet me.

Man, was I nervous. I knew my dad was a no-nonsense-take-care-of-your-duties kind of guy. Sitting across from each other at a corner table, I started my spiel.

"I'm thinking about quitting the pastorate to be a writer. I don't know if I can make a living at it or not...but here's our plan." I explained while he listened and then he responded.

"Well, you don't want to live your life with any I wish I would haves," he said. "You'll do great."

Wilson's don't actually touch each other, but I wanted to lunge across the table and wrap my arms around my dad because that's what you want to do to dream fanners.

Dream fanners aren't enablers (as professional dream killers would like us to believe), they're believers. They believe in God as well as in the dreamer. When my wife or dad encourages my dreams, I hear them say, "I believe in you. I believe you're smart enough, wise enough, clever enough, capable enough, and talented enough to do anything."

But when a dream killer offers their words of wisdom, I hear, "You don't have the brains God gave a goose." They might not mean to convey that, but that's what we dreamers hear.

Ladies, you need to be your husband's dream fanner. If you feel like there's no spark in your marriage...then fan some of his dreams. I've had wives tell me, "But I've killed so many of my husband's dreams that he doesn't dream anymore. What should I do?"

Here's what I suggest: wait. Like a timid rabbit afraid of being gobbled up by a fox, one day your husband will stick his little nose out of his dreaming hole to test the waters. He'll be scared to death to share something, but when he does, you respond with, "I think we should go for it." Then, continue to talk about it and dream WITH him.

Otherwise, he might head right back down his hole.

As a reminder, don't be afraid of the dumb dreams (God will toast them), but as you begin to fan your husband's dreams, he will dream more, and even more importantly, he will dream them with you.

Wives, however, are not the only dream killers on the block. Husbands can be just as guilty.

YOU DON'T WANT
TO GET TO THE END
OF YOUR LIFE WITH
ANY *I WISH I WOULD
HAVES*.

~TODD'S DAD

Dream Killing Hubbys

This isn't always the case, but usually a wife's dream involves family stuff. Things like:

"I'd like to have another child."
"I think we should adopt."
"What about Christian school...homeschool?"
"I feel like we need to be a more spiritual family."
"Our marriage stinks."
"I think we should go on a family trip."

When a husband hears one of those phrases, his brain slips into suspended animation, and he hopes that his silence will divert the conversation to something different.

Fellow dad, sometimes we unwittingly become big, hairy dream killers to our wives. I believe the reason they think about those things is because God has placed a dream in their hearts. We should not only be listening to their voice but cheering them on as well.

When we say things like, "Do we have to talk about that now?" or "I've told you before, we're not going to...," we shut them down, and then wonder why they don't want to be intimate with us. Intimacy is nurtured in the soil of dream fanning.

So men, fan your wife's dreams. Begin by asking your wife, "So, do you still feel strongly about adopting, moving, having another child, taking a family trip or fill in the blank (whatever your wife's dream is)?" Then, just listen or brainstorm with your wife about possible scenarios or the next step to get things rolling.

Kids Have the Scariest Dreams

So far, we've talked about the tendency for wives or husbands to be dream killers, but now let's spend a few moments talking about how parents can end up being the dream killers in their children's lives.

As I mentioned earlier, children come into this world as dreamers, which would be okay with parents if only their dreams weren't so scary. They want to be and do things that only young people could want to be and do.

Usually what happens is that a teenager has a dream (it may or may not have been planted by God) and then shares it with his parents. Then, his mom and dad freak out and quickly take fire control measures, doing their best to stomp out the dream, being careful not to leave the tiniest spark that could possibly re-ignite.

When that happens, the child pulls away from his/her parents. The dream hasn't vanished but now the child knows NOT to share it with them. It becomes a source of contention between them, driving a wedge between parent and child that only deepens as the parent works harder to kill the dream.

As a parent, you need to fan your children's dreams, because children are drawn to people who fan their dreams. As you do, remember God is big enough to kill the dumb dreams.

When my son Ben was 7 or 8 years old, he told me he wanted to own a cruise ship. I don't know where he got the idea. He had never been on a cruise or even seen a single episode of The Love Boat...but he wanted to own a cruise ship.

You know what I didn't do? I never killed that dream. I never said, "A cruise ship? Do you know how much they cost? What kind of mileage do you think they get? Why those are just floating dens of iniquity."

Instead I said, "A cruise ship? That would be so cool!!! You could own it and take me on free rides and we could go anywhere in the world we wanted to."

You know what? My son (now 17) hasn't mentioned owning a cruise ship in years. I'm not even sure he remembers dreaming that. But at the time, I'm sure he loved telling me about his dream because I not only believed in his dream, but more importantly, I believed in him.

Right now, I have another dreamer in my house. My son Ike (10) has the dream of building a jet pack. A while ago, he saw a small blip in God's World magazine about a guy who flew over a mountain with a small jet wing on his back. There was a sparkle in Ike's eye and excitement in his voice when he came up to me, magazine in hand, and thrust it under my nose.

"Dad, look at this," he said. "Do you think we could look on the INTERNET at jet packs?"

"Sure," I answered assuming it wouldn't take long. We looked on YouTube and found a video of the same guy in the magazine article entitled Jet-Man. For nine minutes, we watched the guy jump out of an airplane and blast across the sky.

I figured that would be the last I heard of Jet-Man and rocket packs. I was wrong. A few hours after we had viewed the YouTube video, I happened to see Ike scribbling down his plans for building a jet pack of his own.

"Dad, how much do you think a jet pack costs?" he asked like he was planning a future blast off.

"I'm sure they're super expensive, Ike."

GO FOR IT NOW. THE
FUTURE IS PROMISED
TO NO ONE.

~WAYNE DYER

"But how much?" he asked.

"I don't know, probably at least $10,000."

"Are you sure? Can you check on the INTERNET?" he asked as if the Internet is a magic box that grants you anything you wish.

"Ike," I laughed, "they don't just sell jet engines on eBay."

"Can you check?"

I sighed, "Okay, I'll check." I did a quick Google search and wouldn't you know, the magic box revealed several jet packs you can build for under $200.

It was like throwing gas on a fire. Now for the last week, Ike has been planning to save his money and build a jet pack. I'm sure he envisions himself flying around the backyard above the tree tops with the wind in his face in Superman Style.

I'm a little nervous about the idea of my ten-year-old flying around with a jet-pack strapped to his back. Fortunately, Ike has a little trouble saving money (he sees too many things he likes) so I think I'm safe that it costs $200.

But I don't tell him all that stuff. Instead, I dream with him and cheer him on.

I say, "If anyone could build a jet-pack I think you could, Ike. You're going to be our scientist. When you get your $200 dollars, we'll start building it."

He smiles and so do I. He's a dreamer and loves me for fanning his dreams. His brothers and sister on the other hand are dream killers. They don't intend to be, they just want him to be 'realistic.'

"Like you're going to build a jet-pack, Ike," one brother says.

"You can't save up $10, how are you going to save up $200?" another adds.

"Dad will not let you put a jet-pack on your back," his safe sister says.

But then Ike turns to me to come to his rescue, "Dad, can I build a jet-pack?"

"You bet you can. If anyone can do it...you can. If you save the money, we'll work at building it."

Now, I won't tell him that God might kill this dream because I want my son to know that I believe in him, and who knows... maybe God won't kill it.

The Gift of Believing

I've just given my son one of the greatest gifts a parent can give his child, the gift of believing in him and allowing him to pursue his dream, even if it doesn't look like the kind of dream I would have picked for him.

Some of my sons' dreams aren't necessarily bad or wrong, but my practical father-side of my brain wonders if it will be the best way to provide for his future family. But I know now, that it doesn't matter. It's not just about the best way to provide for a family; it's about dreaming and doing what God has placed in his heart. He'll take care of the providing.

My oldest son has always been a gadget guy. As a little boy, he filled his pockets with little wrenches, pocket knives, and gizmos. We'd walk through a store and he would eye the small do-dads that clicked, blinked, and spun around.

As he got older, he fell in love with technology, laptops, iPods, and cell phones. We were at a Best Buy recently and the employee that he was questioning asked, "How old are you, and why aren't you working here?"

I know he would love that. He knows more about gigabytes and terabytes than anyone I know. He listens to podcasts about the newest phones and future technologies. But here's the deal, I want more for him. I want to push him into something bigger, something respectable where you don't have to wear a bright blue shirt with a yellow logo emblazoned on it.

We've mentioned other IT options but nothing seems to captivate his passion like a phone that can be played like a trombone. He likes gadgets!!

A couple of days ago, as I was driving down some country road, I had a vision of my son as an adult wearing a blue shirt with a yellow logo. He was talking to someone about a cool phone and he was smiling, his heart filled with joy at doing what he loved to do.

I thought then, "That's what he needs to do."

As soon as I thought that, I could almost hear God say, "Just because he starts there doesn't mean I'll have him finish there."

That was comforting...but as I thought more about it I decided that even if he finishes there that's okay because that's what he dreams about.

What a great gift to give your child...the gift of believing, of placing your blessing on his dream. That's what everyone wants but few receive. But not my children and not yours, we're going to let them dream.

FAITH IS THE DARING
OF THE SOUL TO GO
FARTHER THAN IT
CAN SEE.

~NEWTON CLARKE

Fan Early, Fan Often

Not long ago, I was talking to a father whose son wants to be a movie actor. I could tell as we talked that the father is afraid, for a variety of reasons, of what that might lead to. He's tried to get his son to put on the brakes, but his son is pretty sure that's what God wants him to do.

I know the dad fairly well, and from an early age they involved their children in theater. They acted in plays, attended local productions, and spent a lot of time hanging around with theater people. But for some reason, they are surprised that their son wants to be an actor.

Why is that? Didn't they realize that if you intentionally or non-intentionally fan a specific dream, that you shouldn't be surprised when your child wants to carry out that dream?

As a parent you want to intentionally plant certain dreams early on. With my son Ben, I didn't fan his cruise ship dream very seriously. I didn't take him out to the cruise ship dealer to check out our options. Instead, I fanned other dreams...dreams that I believed would be noble dreams and pleasing to God.

Actually, I have specific dreams that I want all my children to dream. For my sons, I want them to dream of being godly fathers and husbands. For my daughters, I want them to dream of being godly wives and mothers.

So, when I see my son Ben holding his little brother up in the air like a plane I say, "Ben, you're going to make a great father one day." I pass Katherine in the kitchen baking something delicious and say, "You're going to be a wonderful wife."

I'm not trying to flatter them...I'm planting and fanning dreams...great dreams...bold dreams...and often times, scary dreams.

But what if your children are no longer dreaming child-like dreams but are in their late teens or early twenties and have dreams that scare you to death? Maybe your son wants to be a drummer in a band or your daughter wants to be a model and move to New York.

In your heart, you know that their 'dream' isn't from God and can't possibly please Him or be good for your child. You try to show your son/daughter the 'light' but that only pushes them away and strengthens their resolve to do it anyway. What's a parent to do then? Fan those 'bad' dreams?

Fan the Dreamer

Now we're treading in deep, choppy water. I'm not going to pretend for one second that this is an easy, one step kind of solution. It's not. But here's what I would advise:

If you can't fan the DREAM, fan the dreamer. You have to find a way to let your child know that you think they've got what it takes to be what they want to be. You need to go to their concert or fashion show and be their biggest fan, clapping louder than anyone and bragging on them.

"You have so much talent...I'm so glad to be your dad...how do you know so much about this stuff?" Remember and cling to the truth that God is big enough to kill dumb dreams. You focus on loving your dreamer.

If you don't and decide instead to take a stand against them, then you will have no influence in their lives. If you can keep them coming back to you, then you can have influence. I don't think you need to put on an act and keep your mouth shut. If they ask for your advice, you should give it.

I know a woman whose husband is involved in a group that she hates and believes is an ungodly group. A while back, he was elected to its highest office and was honored at a big banquet. Sitting at his side was his wife, hating the whole thing, but loving her man.

You tell me what person wouldn't be influenced by a love like that? I just bet one day, he will say to her, "I was a fool...and I love you so much." And even if he doesn't, God is still pleased by the fact that she loved her dreamer anyway.

That's a dream fanner.

OK, let's get back to the original story.

Turn Away

David took the first dream killer's shot between the eyes and was still standing. I can just see Eliab and his two brothers staring at their kid brother with a 'take that' in their eyes.

A non-dreamer would have responded with, "You're right. What was I thinking? Thanks guys...have a biscuit."

But not David. He was a dreamer just like you, and he did what I would encourage you to do when you're confronted by a dream killer—he turned away. That's what you should do when

It often requires
more courage to
dare to do right
than to fear to do
wrong.

~Abraham Lincoln

someone tells you have no business even thinking about what you're thinking—plug your ears and turn away.

Don't listen to their loud voices. If you believe God has put a dream in your heart...turn away.

The Bible tells us that David turned away and again asked those around him, "So what will be done for the guy who kills the giant?"

Apparently surrounded by lily-livered cowards, David's question made a big splash and shortly after, David finds himself summoned by the king. Now scripture doesn't record where the meeting took place, but I picture it taking place near the King's tent surrounded by all his royal groupies and body guards.

Standing before King Saul was a handsome young man dressed as a shepherd. I wonder if Saul's expression betrayed his doubt, because David is recorded as speaking first.

"Cheer up," he said with confidence. "Don't worry, I'll fight him."

I can't even begin to imagine what Saul thought (and I have a pretty good imagination). Here he was surrounded by the green berets of the Israelite army and no one had yet accepted Goliath's challenge. Now, this baby-faced youth standing before him said with confidence that he'd go and fight the giant.

But there's one thing David didn't count on...he was about to encounter another dream killer.

A Royal Dream Killer

It's important to remember when battling dream killers that they travel in packs, like zombies on a video game. Just when you think you've defeated one, another takes its place.

David turned away from one dream killer and ran into a bigger one...an expert that looks at situations realistically and quotes statistics.

"You? You want to fight the giant? Are you nuts? You are not able to go out against this giant. You are just a youth. He has been a warrior since he was a youth!" the expert argued.

Isn't that the way it is with some dream killers? They love to remind us of others who have failed doing what we are attempting to do. They like to point out the economics of the situation, the odds, and the failures.

"How are you going to afford that?"

"Don't you know that it will cost $53,000 a year to send your child to college when they reach that age?"

"I heard about a couple that adopted a child who murdered them in their sleep and then ATE them!!"

The temptation is to try to calm their fears by spouting off abilities, assuring the dream killer that 'you can handle it.' That's a mistake and a battle that cannot be won. The truth is that God-sized dreams can't be accomplished by ANYONE, but God.

David knew that and as he related his past successes to King Saul, he made it crystal clear that all his past and future successes were because of God.

*"Your servant was tending his father's sheep. When
a lion or a bear came and took a lamb from the flock, I
went out after him and attacked him, and rescued it from
his mouth; and when he rose up against me, I seized him
by his beard and struck him and killed him.*

*Your servant has killed both the lion and the bear;
and this uncircumcised Philistine will be like one of them,
since he has taunted the armies of the living God." And
David said, "The LORD who delivered me from the paw
of the lion and from the paw of the bear, He will deliver
me from the hand of this Philistine."* (1 Samuel 17:36,
37a)

Yes, that's the ticket, David...God can do it. And God is the
accomplisher of your dreams as well. Why? Because He's the
Dream Giver and fulfiller.

So to the person who says, "You want another child? How
are you going to pay for it when you can barely afford the ones
you have right now?"

You say, "The Bible says that children are a blessing from
God...they are a gift from Him. I believe that if God wants to give
us a good gift, He will also take care of us."

To the dream killer who says, "The economy is terrible right
now, why would you leave a high paying job just so you can spend
more time with your family?" you say, "God says I'm supposed to
train my children when they rise up, lie down, and when they walk
along the road...and I can't do that if I'm at work all the time. If
that is the truth...then God will take care of us."

A Christian dream killer won't be able to argue.

They know their Bibles. They know the verses that talk about

PRUDENCE KEEPS
LIFE SAFE, BUT DOES
NOT OFTEN MAKE IT
HAPPY.

~SAMUEL JOHNSON

trusting God, His provision for our needs, not storing up treasures on earth, and living without fear...they just don't live it.

When a dream killer realizes his approach is not working he might quickly changes tactics.

"Go," Saul said, "and may the LORD be with you." In my mind, I see a slight smile curl on the edge of his mouth.

Dream Manipulators

"Hey David," Saul 'probably' called out, "I see you're not wearing any armor. No one goes to battle without it. You won't last three seconds if you don't have some protection. Tell you what; I'll let you wear MINE."

I'm just sure David was flattered that the king would loan him HIS royal armor. In my mind I picture the climax in the second Lord of the Rings movie when Théoden, king of Rohan stands in a large room backlit by an open doorway. His captain at arms straps his gleaming golden armor to his body as ominous music plays.

In the same fashion, Saul's armor was carried in and strapped onto the brave dreamer. There was no music, but I'm sure David felt strong, secure, and invincible.

Now I don't know if they had mirrors back then, but I can imagine David puffed up and looking buff as he gazed at the fierce-looking warrior staring back at him from the mirror.

Then, I wonder if he heard a gentle whisper deep in his heart that said, "David, what are you doing, boy? This is not you, nor the way I want you to go meet the giant."

If dream killers can't kill your dream outright, then they will try to manipulate you to do it THEIR way. They don't do it to be mean; they just can't imagine NOT doing it in the way that makes the most sense.

For Saul, it was the idea that you don't go to battle without wearing armor. For the dream killers that surround you, it will be something different but just as 'reasonable.'

> *"Well, if you want another baby will you at least talk to a doctor to see how safe it is at YOUR age?"*
>
> *"If you're going into the ministry, you'll need to go to seminary first."*
>
> *"How about meeting with my financial adviser before you quit your job and start a home business?"*
>
> *"If you feel like you need to homeschool, make sure you at least have the kids tested regularly."*

I've met these types of dream manipulators. I was speaking to a large audience of men in Minnesota when a flashy, charismatic guy came up to me.

"You do an incredible job communicating truths," he said, "but I know a way you can sell more books and make more money."

Now I certainly didn't go into the business of encouraging parents to make a lot of money...but the idea of making more money sounded pretty good at the moment so I asked him, "And, how would you do that?"

He went on to tell me that he was a motivational business speaker and what he found successful was a technique that he had used to sell gobs of books. "It's simple," he said. "All you do at the end of your presentation is say, *now I think I brought enough books for all of you, but you'll want to hurry right out to my product table to make sure you get a copy.* I'm telling you, it works" he said with excitement.

Well, I liked the idea of selling more books and making more money so as I wound down my presentation to the group, I said, "Now I think I brought enough books for all of you, but you'll want to hurry right out to my product table to make sure you get a copy."

As soon as the words left my mouth, I felt like a big, fake idiot. The truth is I have no business savvy. I'm not sophisticated or slick. In fact, I'm even kind of shlocky...but that's the way I'm supposed to be and the way God wants me to do the dream He has placed in my heart.

You know what? I've never tried that guy's book selling technique again...although I do think I have enough copies of this book for all of your friends...so you'll want to make sure...

Remember my friend Mark? That's what he's discovered. In fact, he wrote just a few minutes ago.

> *Todd,*
>
> *I have been trying to talk with other Christians in order to gather wise counsel about making a change and working independently. I am met with varying degrees but all slanted in the same direction...don't do anything hastily, you have to plan, things take time, consider your savings cushion vs. time to profitability, etc. None are as encouraging as you.*
>
> *What I get are conventional business practices— feasibility studies and business plan activities...*

IF YOU DON'T MAKE
MISTAKES, IT'S
BECAUSE YOU'RE NOT
DOING ANYTHING.

~TODD'S DAD

Let's all take a tip from David's life. Notice that David didn't say, "You want me to try on your armor? No way!!!! I'm going to do it my way or no way. You can take your armor, Oh King, and sell it on eBay!!!"

David was wise beyond his years by trying on the armor, swinging the sword, and hefting the shield...but when it didn't feel right, he was wiser still to set it aside.

Go ahead and meet with advisers, read books, listen to ideas, and try on their armor...BUT, and this is a big BUT, if it doesn't feel right, set it aside. God has made you smart enough to do His dream His way...and He will make it clear what His way is.

The dream killers in your life will not understand your decisions...but who cares? Their jaws will drop and their heads will nod in disapproval (I assume Saul's eyes popped out of his royal head when David removed his armor)...BUT WHO CARES?!! Your job is to do what you believe God would have you do...the WAY He would have you do it.

Crazy Dreamers

I bet you could have heard a pin drop as David removed his last piece of armor, picked up his staff, and made his way to the nearest brook to pick out a few stones for his sling shot.

How stupid was that? He was about to face a giant with a stick and some rocks!!! Everyone knows that's not how it is done.

But that is what made David a dreamer and why it was recorded in the Bible. The account probably would have been omitted if it had been a bigger guy who killed Goliath with a bigger sword. But the account of David and Goliath was recorded for you and me because it is not about swords, championship warriors, or even the dreamer...it's about GOD.

Be a Rock Chucker

Let's linger a moment at the brook where David chose his FIVE smooth stones. Because we've been indoctrinated by Dennis the Menace, we picture a sling shot cut from a 'y' shaped tree branch crotch. Between the arms, we imagine an old innertube rubberband along with a few marble-sized rocks for ammunition.

Wipe that picture from your mind.

David's sling shot was a long, leather-strapped sling that was swung in a circle like a...a...sling shot. The stones used were not marble-sized but baseball-sized. The Dennis the Menace sling shot might kill a pigeon; the David kind of sling shot could kill a...giant.

It intrigues me that the Bible recorded that he chose FIVE stones. Why do you think he chose that number?

Some Biblical authorities would argue that Goliath had four sons (1 Samuel 21:22) and I guess they think that David would have popped them off if they caused him any trouble. Now they might be right...but I don't think so.

My theory is pretty simple: I think that if David missed with his first rock, he was going to reach into his pouch and launch another. If that one missed, he was going to fire off another. I believe this dreamer was going to chuck rocks until either the giant was dead or he was out of rocks. I'm not sure what he planned to do after that, but I don't think he had a plan B.

That's another mark of a dreamer: he doesn't quit if he misses with his first rock. He quickly reloads and tries again.

I once read that Walt Disney went bankrupt seven times, that Thomas Edison had 3,000 failures before he invented the incandescent light bulb, that the Wright brothers crashed more than their fare share of airplanes before their first successful flight, and that honest Abe lost his first race for a political office.

I know of plenty of dreamers who shared their great idea with the world and no one cared. They were turned away, turned down, and told to give up. But they didn't. Dreamers never do...because they're rock chuckers.

I get emails from dreamers who share their dream with me and then go on to say how they tried it, but it didn't work like they thought it might, and they quit.

"So what?" I want to tell them. "Don't give up so easily just because your first rock landed a little off target. Reach in your bag and chuck another rock."

Don't think that your dream will be easy! Real dreams are never easy. They rarely go according to plan, and often lead to brick walls and frustration. If dreaming was easy, everyone would be dreamers...there would have been a mile long line of volunteers to fight the giant.

Dreams are dangerous, potentially disastrous, and sometimes end in death. The Bible is filled with dreamers who were beaten, broken, and crucified. Non-dreamers and dream killers sip lemonade

IT'S KIND OF FUN TO
DO THE IMPOSSIBLE.

~WALT DISNEY

and watch ESPN from their comfortable couches in their comfortable houses, while enjoying their comfortable lives.

Dreamer, your dream will not be easy to accomplish. It may not go just like you think. You may have to humble yourself and do things you'd rather not do. It may take longer than you think, and you just might FAIL and have to eat crow.

But that's OK...because you're a DREAMER!!!!!

Remember my friend, Mark? In another recent email, he wrote:

> *Todd, if I were single and didn't have a family to take care of, I could be dangerous...I could do it (his dream).*

I responded and said, "Mark, if you were single and didn't have a family...that would be SAFE. What makes you a dreamer is that it is not safe."

I know plenty of young men and women, who start up a business, go to college, or have children. That's safe.

But for the person who is already 43, with a family of four, who starts a business, goes to college, or has more children, now that's dangerous...scary dangerous. And that's what makes him/her a dreamer.

Dreams Aren't as Scary as They Seem

However, many times a dream, or a giant, isn't as hard or as tough as it first seems. Maybe Goliath wasn't as invincible as most people thought. Maybe he was past his prime and relied on his size to intimidate. We don't know, but we DO know that David figured it might take up to five rocks to pop off this guy and it only took one.

I know in my own life that what I often think will be a terrible situation turns out to be much easier than all the dream killers warned me it would be.

Just last year I was asked to speak in Hawaii. Thinking it might be a great family opportunity, we decided that the whole Wilson bunch (all ten of us plus a niece) would make the trip.

You should have seen the looks and heard the horror stories about how difficult it would be to fly with children, let alone EIGHT! Most suggested we leave some of them behind.

Somewhere early on in the process, we began to doubt our idea of a great family time and re-designed our trip with various numbers of children...just the oldest...everyone except the three youngest...none. Finally, we decided, "*We're a family. We do things as a family. We can't imagine seeing the sights without all of us together. We're all going. Besides, if we wanted easy we wouldn't have had a family.*"

As we tooled through the various airport terminals, we looked like a cross between the Brady Bunch and the Clampett's. Heads turned and mouths counted the number in our party. I'm sure some (or most) thought we were crazy.

But you know what? It wasn't that bad. Actually, I'm still amazed by how smoothly it went, AND we all went to Hawaii. We all have the memory of shave ice at Matsumoto's, watching a monk seal swim up to the beach, snorkeling, and enjoying the beach right out our back door.

I know a family who has been dreaming about traveling abroad with their family for years. They have saved the money... they just don't know if they can work out all of the details. They see the giant as TWENTY feet tall instead of what it actually is...a small hurdle to overcome.

Giants are deceptive. They yell and holler and stand up tall on their tip toes, but I think their foreheads are made of china, and they go down easily.

The same is true for your dream. It probably won't be as hard to achieve as you think it will, but you'll never find out if you stay in the shallows.

Be like David. Pick out your rocks and walk to meet the giant. I'm sure King Saul, David's brothers, and the entire Israelite army watched on in silence as David stepped out of the camp and made his way onto the battlefield. Some thought he would die, most thought he was nuts, and ALL wished they had the guts to do what he was about to attempt.

The Deadliest Dream Killer of All

Continue imagining the scene: one large valley and two hills on opposite sides filled with soldiers, banners, and excitement. We don't know exactly how it played out, but I believe Goliath came out from his tent as he had for the last forty days to give his daily challenge.

As he stepped out from the ranks of the Philistine line, he saw a solitary man standing in the center of the valley. Did his body

THE PERSON WHO
GOES FARTHEST IS
GENERALLY THE ONE
WHO IS WILLING TO
DO AND DARE. THE
SURE-THING BOAT
NEVER GETS FAR
FROM SHORE.

~DALE CARNEGIE

pulse with adrenaline and his heart beat faster? Did he feel the fear of a bully who was being challenged or could he taste the blood of a soon to be victim?

The sound must have been deafening as each side cheered, and the distance between the champion and the dreamer closed. I assume that David stopped somewhere along the way as the giant advanced. Shocked by what became clearer the closer he got, Goliath looked over his opponent and instead of seeing a warrior worthy of battle he saw a boy...handsome and ruddy.

"Am I a dog," Goliath shouted at David, "that you come at me with sticks?" Like a heavy-weight prize fighter who just found out he is going to fight a cub scout instead of a contender, Goliath cursed David, the day, and all his enemies.

"Come here, you young maggot, and I'll give your flesh to the birds of the air and the beast of the field," Goliath bellowed.

As David faced his formidable opponent, from the darkest shadows arose one final dream killer that had the power to suck the life from even the bravest dreamer.

The Granddaddy of Dream Killers

Surely David must have gasped at Goliath's enormous size. From a distance, he looked big...but up close he was colossal, with arms and legs like timbers, a chest like a barrel, and murderous eyes like coals of fire.

It's not actually recorded in Scripture, but I'm convinced that somewhere in the blank space between the end of verse 44

(1 Samuel 17) and the beginning of verse 45, David met the most deadly of all dream killers...himself.

As David stood in the shadow of this ten foot tall giant, I'm guessing he thought, "They're ALL right. I have no business fighting giants...what am I doing...I'm going to die and this is really going to hurt."

Obviously, David didn't know...the song.

> *Only a boy named David, only a little sling*
> *Only a boy named David, but he could play and*
> *sing.*
> *Only a boy named David, only a rippling brook*
> *Only a boy named David, and five little stones he*
> *took.*
> *And one little stone went into the sling and the sling*
> *went round and round*
> *One little stone went into the sling and the sling*
> *went round and round*
> *And round and round and round and round and*
> *round and round and round*
> *And one little stone went into the airrrr...**and the***
> ***giant came tumbling downnnn.***

Since David didn't know that song, he didn't know that it would only take one stone. He didn't know that the giant was going to tumble down. Oh, he believed that God had given the giant into his hand...but he didn't **know**.

And that's what made him a dreamer. Because dreamers do what they do without knowing how the 'song' ends.

Little Mouse...Big Dreamer

One of my favorite dreamers is a fictitious dreamer. You can find him in the third book of the Chronicles of Narnia. He stands just two feet tall, is covered in black fur, and is always volunteering to be sent into battle, fight dragons, or to go on suicide missions.

You probably guessed it, but I'm talking about Reepicheep, the talking mouse.

He makes it into a couple of C.S. Lewis's volumes, but my favorite appearance is the one he makes in "*Prince Caspian and the Voyage of the Dawn Treader*." The whole premise of the story is that an older Prince Caspian sets sail in search of seven Lords who have been missing for years.

During the course of the book, Caspian and the rest of the crew encounter many adventures, but they eventually account for all seven lords. Towards the end of the tale, the crew has gathered on deck to discuss their next move. They've already sailed further than any living soul and fear they may be getting close to the edge of the world.

Let's listen in on the conversation that took place.

The voice we hear is Drinian's, the Captain.

"I can't understand this. There is not a breath of wind. The sail hangs dead. The sea is as flat as a pond. And yet we drive on as fast as if there were a gale behind us."

"I've been thinking that, too," said Caspian. "We must be caught in some strong current."

"H'm," said Edmund. "That's not so nice if the World really has an edge and we're getting near it."

IF I HAD MY LIFE TO LIVE
OVER AGAIN, I'D DARE TO
MAKE MORE MISTAKES THE
NEXT TIME.

~NADINE STAIR

"You mean," said Caspian, "that we might be just—well, poured over it?"

Now a squeaky voice pipes in.

"Yes, yes," cried Reepicheep, clapping his paws together. "That's how I've always imagined it—the World like a great round table and the waters of all the oceans endlessly pouring over the edge. The ship will tip up—stand on her head—for one moment we shall see over the edge—and then, down, down, the rush, the speed—"

"And what do you think will be waiting for us at the bottom, eh?" said Drinian.

"Aslan's country, perhaps," said the Mouse, his eyes shining. "Or perhaps there isn't any bottom. Perhaps it goes down for ever and ever. But whatever it is, won't it be worth anything just to have looked for one moment beyond the edge of the world?"

That little mouse...is one big dreamer.

I get goosebumps every time I read that passage and pray that I can be that brave. I've known plenty of people who have been. They may not have sailed beyond the edge of the world, but they sailed into unknown waters not knowing if they would sail right off the edge of the world.

My dad did that when he left the school system and started his little print shop. My mid-fifty-year old friends, Bill and Joyce, did that when they adopted an eight-year-old girl from Taiwan. Joey did so when he left his good-paying job to start a ministry to encourage dads.

Moms have done so when they pulled their children out of school to homeschool them. Dads have done that when they left their jobs to go to seminary, work out of their homes, or go to some village in Tanzania to share the Gospel.

Like Reepicheep, none of them knew how the adventure would end but they set sail just the same. Unfortunately, I can't tell you that if you act on your dream then it will all end happily ever after. I can't tell you that if you leave your job to work at home that you'll make it.

I can't tell you that if you adopt, that child won't break your heart one day. I can't tell you that you won't end up on the jagged rocks below. I don't know...but you can find out.

In another great Chronicles of Narnia book, *Prince Caspian*, Lucy failed to follow Aslan, the great lion, because the other children didn't believe she had really seen him. Later she meets Aslan and talks to him about her failure.

> *"You mean," said Lucy rather faintly, "that it would have turned out all right—somehow? But how? Please, Aslan! Am I not to know?"*
> *"To know what **would** have happened," said Aslan. "No. Nobody is ever told that."*
> *"Oh dear," said Lucy.*
> *"But anyone can find out what **will** happen," said Aslan.*

Did you hear that? Aslan is so right. You don't know what **might** happen if you step out and dream big, but you can find out what **will** happen if you go for it. I don't know if it will have a happy ending or a less than happy ending, BUT won't it be worth anything just to have looked for one moment beyond the edge of the world?

Time is running out.

The Reason for This Book

Let me tell you about Marty. Marty talked to me while I was speaking in Florida at a large homeschool convention about five years ago. As we talked, he told me that he travels a lot and is away from his family several days a week.

"Just this past week, "he said, "I found a note tucked into my wallet from my seven-year-old son." He paused as though he was looking at it in his mind. "It said, *Dad, please come home*."

"I know I'm blowing it, Todd," he said, "but I don't know what to do."

"That's easy," I said. "Quit."

He looked at me like I had worms hanging from my nose. "Quit? But I don't have another plan."

"Well, don't keep doing something you know to be wrong just because you don't have another plan." I didn't say it, but anyone would quit his job if he could step right into another well-paying job.

"Do you know how scary that is?" he asked.

"Oh, I know it's scary, Marty...but you need to do it."

"But what will I do?"

"I don't know...but do it anyway."

That was five years ago. Four years ago Marty came up to me again. He was still working at the job he had the year before but knew he should quit.

"Then do it, Marty. Time's running out."

"Do you know that everyone else I've asked says I'd be crazy to leave this great job?"

FACE YOUR FEAR AND
SADDLEUP ANYWAY!

~JOHN WAYNE

"Everyone else is wrong!!!" I said a little more urgently, "Just do it."

"But it's scary."

"Of course it's scary...but do it!!"

That was four years ago. Three years ago he came up again and things had not changed. He was hesitant and I encouraged him to quit.

I haven't seen him since, but I know he still has the same type of job. And he has lost five more years of his family's life.

Here's the deal...five years turns into a lifetime just like (snap) that. That's why I'm pleading with you to DO IT!!! Don't put off your dream because it probably won't get any easier. Just do it. Quit looking at the size of the giant and remember the size of your God. Do it!!!! Quit worrying about what might happen and find out what WILL happen. Do it!!!!

Run to Meet the Giant

Since David believed how big God was, the account of David and Goliath didn't stop after verse 44 with David walking back to the Israelite army.

Listen to his battlefield monologue. It began a bit subdued, but by the end David was shouting in confidence, not about his ability but about God's.

> *"You come to me with a sword, a spear, and a javelin, but I come to you in the name of the LORD of hosts, the God of the armies of Israel, whom you have taunted.*

> *This day the LORD will deliver you up into my*
> *hands, and I will strike you down and remove your head*
> *from you. And I will give the dead bodies of the army of*
> *the Philistines this day to the birds of the sky and the wild*
> *beasts of the earth, that all the earth may know that there*
> *is a God in Israel, and that all this assembly may know*
> *that the LORD does not deliver by sword or by spear; for*
> *the battle is the LORD'S and He will give you into our*
> *hands."* (1 Samuel 17:45-47)

Tired of talk, Goliath moved to attack David. David was done listening to dream killers (even himself) and ran to meet the giant. Man, I love that part. He may have been scared a few minutes before but now he was moving. It didn't matter what anyone else said or what he felt, or how it would end...he just ran to meet the giant.

That's what you need to do. Don't hesitate...RUN to meet YOUR giant. Set your last day at work, draw up your resignation, get the adoption papers, talk to your spouse, draw up a plan, call the travel agent, or do whatever it takes to get the ball rolling.

So David reached into his pouch, picked out a stone, and the stone went into the sling and...round and round and round...and one little stone went into the airrrr....and the giant came tumbling down. The rest is history.

David grabbed Goliath's mammoth sword and cut off his opponent's head...just to be sure. Then, do you know what he did with Goliath's weapons? The Scripture says he placed them in his tent. Now we don't know for sure, but I bet he placed them next to the skin of a lion and the skin of a bear to serve as reminders, not only of dreaming big but also of God's power.

People didn't live in homes back then but in tents. We read in the Bible that David moved around a lot. When he did, he had to take everything out of his tent, fold up his tent, and then do it in reverse when he got to his next campsite.

I assume that Goliath's weapons went with him. And I assume that every once in a while when David was minding his own business God whispered in his heart, "David, I've got something I want you to do."

I'm sure it was scary and wasn't safe. But I would guess that when he went back to his tent that old giant's weapons caught his eye. Next to them sat a lion and bear skin, and I bet he thought, *God delivered me from the paw of the lion, the paw of the bear, AND the hand of the giant...bring it on God.*

So, my fellow dreamer, go and do likewise. Quit listening to the dream killers in your life and follow your God-given dream. Don't listen to your fears or your doubts...do it. Don't worry about how it *might* end...Do it and find out how it *will* end. And, remember to fan the dreams of those around you.

Together, let's DREAM BIG!

PS: Tell me how it turns out. Send your story to me at:
familyman@bnin.net

Voice of Truth
by Casting Crowns

Oh, what I would do to have
the kind of faith it takes
To climb out of this boat I'm in
Onto the crashing waves
To step out of my comfort zone
Into the realm of the unknown
Where Jesus is,
And he's holding out his hand

But the waves are calling out my name
and they laugh at me
Reminding me of all the times
I've tried before and failed
The waves they keep on telling me
time and time again
"Boy, you'll never win,
You will never win."

But the Voice of truth tells me a different story
the Voice of truth says "do not be afraid!"
and the Voice of truth says "this is for My glory"
Out of all the voices calling out to me
I will choose to listen and believe the Voice of truth

Oh, what I would do
to have the kind of strength it takes
To stand before a giant
with just a sling and a stone
Surrounded by the sound
of a thousand warriors
shaking in their armor
Wishing they'd have had the strength to stand

But the giant's calling out
my name and he laughs at me
Reminding me of all the times
I've tried before and failed
The giant keeps on telling me
time and time again
"Boy you'll never win,
you'll never win."

But the voice of truth tells me a different story
the Voice of truth says "do not be afraid!"
and the Voice of truth says "this is for My glory"
Out of all the voices calling out to me
I will choose to listen and believe the Voice of truth

But the stone was just the right size
to put the giant on the ground
and the waves they don't seem so high
from on top of them looking down
I will soar with the wings of eagles
when I stop and listen to the sound of Jesus
singing over me

But the Voice of truth tells me a different story
The Voice of truth says "do not be afraid!"
And the Voice of truth says "this is for my glory"
Out of all the voices calling out to me (calling out to me)
I will choose to listen and believe
(I will choose to listen and believe)
I will choose to listen and believe the Voice of truth

I will listen and believe
I will listen and believe the Voice of truth
I will listen and believe
'Cause Jesus you are the Voice of truth
And I will listen to you... oh you are the Voice of truth

Amen

T odd Wilson and his beautiful, dream-fanning wife have eight, sometimes adorable, dreamers of their own. Together, they travel the country in a big RV encouraging parents. They make their home in Northern Indiana and go out for pizza and breadsticks on Sunday nights. Todd is also the founder of Family-man Ministries, whose purpose is to remind YOU of what's most important.

To have Todd speak at your group or to check out his other great resources for parents, go to **www.familymanweb.com**.